First published in 2025 by PRESS DIONYSUS LTD in the UK, 167 Portland Road, N15 4SZ, London.

www.pressdionysus.com

Paperback

ISBN 978-1-0361617-1-5
Copyright © 2025 by PRESS DIONYSUS

All rights reserved. Printed in the UK. No part of this book may be used or reproduced in any manner whatsoever without written permission except in the case of brief quotations embodied in critical articles or reviews.

First published in 2025 by PRESS DIONYSUS LTD in the UK, 167, Portland Road, N15 4SZ, London.

www.pressdionysus.com

Paperback

ISBN: 978-1-913961-49-7
Copyright © 2025 by PRESS DIONYSUS.

Love, Hate and Fragility

Tony Howson

DIONYSUS

ISBN- 978-1-913961-49-7
© Press Dionysus 2025

Copyright for all text: Tony Howson

Copyright for cover design: Tony Howson

Press Dionysus LTD, 167, Portland Road, N15 4SZ, London
- e-mail: info@pressdionysus.com
- web: www.pressdionysus.com

The poet:

Born in Slough in 1956, Tony Howson fulfilled his childhood dream to travel, visiting a total 140 countries, working for BBC and BBC Media Action. Much of his work was around designing and making programmes on taboo subjects, as well as training in-country journalists to carry them on. Primarily he worked in regions affected by conflict and poverty, including Somalia, Sierra Leone, Libya, Ukraine and Gaza. Now retired from journalism, he continues to write and teach English. He has published two previous collections of poetry and essays, The Crow Road from Eden (Valley Press) and Walking with Camels (Dionysus Press), as well as contributing to various collections. He has also trained others in the art of storytelling, leading to performance nights. Tony has performed his own work in the UK and overseas.

Tony's poetry reflects his experiences with extensive travel to "remote and often dangerous" places. His work is described as a mix of poetry, prose, and pictures, which he uses to make sense of the world. The themes in his work include personal and global events, and the reflection on "minefields of madness."

His writing, which includes verse and prose, is said to be imbued with a "reporter's awareness of truths— political and human." The work can be elliptical in poetry and pointed in prose, covering topics such as "concentration camps, prisons, rigged elections, sunrises and sunsets, sorrow, dancing and love." He is described as a person who has "stared into the flames," but also someone who is not afraid to talk about the "soul" or to celebrate simple pleasures like a meal with friends.

In this book we experience love and hate through the components of emotional expression.

Love, Hate and Fragility
An introduction

Love is the rabbit in the moon. Love is red roses. Love is a box of bitter chocolates, with one space filled by a pair of diamond earrings. Love is a profound and multifaceted emotion that encompasses a wide range of feelings, states, and attitudes. It is often characterised by deep affection, protectiveness, intimacy and a strong desire for connection and well- being.

Hate is the stark opposite. Hate is an intense, negative response. Typically, it is directed towards a person, group, object, or idea. Its roots grow in intense dislike or aversion. It shows hostility, anger, resentment, contempt, and disgust. That leads to devaluation, fear, and insecurity. Hate is that coiled metal spring that builds, clenches and pings in sudden, out-of-control frenzy.

They can be opposites, or, as some see it, divided by a thin line. And that is where fragility sits. That is the space of fear of failure, passion and all-consuming emotions. Intense love, intense hate, plays on the fragility, the insecurity stimulated by both. But the intention of love and hate emotions remains fundamentally different: one to uplift, the other to tear down.

And the triggers that fuel fragility could be as simple as the question posed by that space where the diamond earrings sit: Who ate the chocolate?

We find love and hate in war and peace. We find it in our intimate relations. We find it on different levels in many places. Sometimes its work. Often it is like the playground see-saw we play on, some imbalance tips the scale, and one end comes down with a bump.

Some things just get left to fate's invisible hand at the dice table. The dice roll in different directions, culminating in a result that could never be foreseen. Our choices ride on the grand toss of fate. Lose and you deal with the result. But know this: the dice do not care what you want.

I am never sure what I think about love. We go shopping for it down the high street, see something that fits our need at that time, try it on and then, maybe, buy it. But like that pair of expensive jeans, our body changes with gluttonous lifestyle. The fit no longer matches our curves, which now overhang.

With love, you work it out, and move on to good but revised times. Or hate sets in. Body shamed, you get out and make sure the blame lands not on you. Resentment and contempt can come in to play, and from there, other negative feelings bubble up. Often the zip breaks at this point. And you know which zip I mean. The front of those jeans, or that nice party dress that suddenly slips to the floor.

In a world of more than eight billion people, we find love in our known habitat. Love, I guess, is about committing to grow together. But then surroundings change. I am never sure if love is about the long term, as it is meant to be in its purified state, or just about the time and place we are in at a given moment in life. Often love is about what personal security you take from, or give to, the other person.

Actor Ian McKellen said we should all call each other love, never mind the pronouns, and gender battles. But we cannot really love everyone, can we?

Hate is a lot simpler. You just hate the other, the one or one million you can blame for all the bad things in life. And the one who questions love at a given time can be a good target. A possible recruit for hate.

Many love to say: "I love this person so much". Sometimes they mean it. But not many admit to hate, just to being right. Love can be blind in some respects but hate blinds itself. It is that imbalance on the see-saw. The other has what we want. The other wants what we want. One side may reflect hate, but the other can hate in return because love is threatened.

How many times have you heard the phrase: "I am not racist." Then follows the "but these people should not come here, taking our jobs." Then of course there is "I am not anti-Gay, but it is disgusting seeing them holding hands in public."

One can afford to buy diamond earrings for their loved ones, but others cannot. Perhaps that is why we cannot love the world. Some have what others want. Others can only choose to want it, but cannot have it. That is how the world is. That is a source of jealousy or injustice.

We live in a world of false choices. You may want a Porsche Boxster, but as some rich guy drives away the last unaffordable one in the showroom. You can only choose the left-over Toyota Yaris. It was never a real choice.

But in all these false choices, there are things we desire, or would love to have, but cannot because the foundation for owning them is not with us. Thus, the pot of hate gets stirred.

Such is the joy, the excitement when a box of chocolates gets delivered to your door. Open it and you find one empty space. No diamond earrings, and one chocolate down. Expectations maybe high, disappointment is deep.

There are of course many different viewpoints. Friends sent feedback on this book:

"I have to say that I'm not a 'love' person. To me, all this talk of love seems rather like commercialised existentialism."

"I don't think love is fragile. I think it's smart packaging: shiny, customisable, highly flammable. It is the system's best bait. It keeps people dreaming, distracted and shopping."

"And as for hate? At least it doesn't pretend. You know where you stand with hate. Love shows up like a grand production. Once the mystery goes, you're just left with someone else's habits and the realisation that maybe it was hormones, not soulmates."

"The sentence, "Love can be blind in some ways," re-minded me of a similar sentence in a book I read, "Love is a state of selective blindness." It's another good observation. The sentence, "Hate blinds itself," also emphasises this destructive and uncontrolled emotion."

"I guess it would be nice to get a box of chocolates with a diamond once in a while."

Shush!

The world is Bedlam.
A whirlpool of madness.
Swirling white heat.
Searing flesh.

World turned like
The Minch boiling,
Morpheus churning,
Millpond to maelstrom.

This is where it all started,
In a phosphorus flash
Amidst the home front rubble.
Smoke choking dust, settling layers
Upon the brick turned to brimstone.

Twisted iron fences, contorting, snagging
Life's forgotten ordinary things:
      A teddy bear
                    A shirt
                          A bra
A clutching hand that could not hold on.
 Lost

Amongst the blood-stained bricks.
A woman not just blown apart,
But stoned to her death.
Silence cradles the vaporised body,
A stunned spirit wrapped in a dust cloud.
Nothing more.

The weeping working man

I knew he was a working man.
His fingers thick, hands rough,
And creases on his face,
Older than his years.
The blackness of oil and grime
Ingrained.
He rolls his own cigarettes,
Nicotine stains on his fingers,
Stain upon stain.

I watched him weep.
Tears left streaks down his cheeks.
Those hardened hands,
Knuckles white,
Clutched the bra,
The Teddy Bear,
The shirt.
The bra those rough fingers once unclipped
To feel warm flesh with a loving care.

I watched his love
Turn to hate.
In the dampness of his heavy eyes,

There was a flame that flared
The colour of the furnace
Where his thoughts and dreams were thrown.
As if he could strangle and butcher
In a sweat, so cold,
His Hell was revenge.

Soul

My mother's soul lives in a vase
Once filled with plastic roses
Picked from sellotape, stuck
To the sides of washing up packets.
Each rose of red or yellow
Gave her simple joy
When plucked and placed
Inside the vase.

Like all picked roses,
They faded into a memory
Stronger,
      More lasting,
           Than plastic.

If death takes me into that vase,
Keep it safe.
Ignore its fault lines and cracks,
Just have a good memory
Where love reunites lost souls.

The mystery of home

I have never known home.
But I have looked for it,
Under stones found on a beach.
Behind walls with collapsed roofs.
In cupboards where mice build nests.

Do not, I beg you,
Compare me to a refugee,
For at least they have a starting point.
Nor should I be compared to a wandering Jew.
They had a dream for a place to go.

I have fooled myself with cliches,
Laying down my hat for a while.
But it never managed to stay off my head,
Until I had a dream, a little wet perhaps,
As I lay naked on a bed.

I dreamt you came to me,
Whoever you are,
And lay next to me, in silence.
You had the courage to arrive naked
And left wearing the same clothes.

You never returned,
And loneliness grew deeper.

Loneliness drives you mad

Loneliness drives you mad.
But it depends
On what makes you lonely.
The lowest point is the loneliness
That emerges ghost like
From inside love.

Viscous liquid seeps slowly through
the spongy outer walls, and,
With time, its inexorable presence
Seeps to the inner side,
The blind side that only the lonely
Can see.

It's sallow stain emerges
Like a bruise, and ages
To yellow, dark blue,
Brown like taffy it drips
And drips as if you are there,

Inside a crowded room,
Laying on a camp bed,
Cold, sweating a haunting fever.

Everyone sees you,
the physical dancer,
But that inner space
Remains latent to outside eyes.

"See me" screams
in your isolated head,
Strapped to the bed
As drop, drip, drop
Taps your forehead.

Your ears cannot stop
The muffled sound
On the other side
Of that porous wall.

I love you now,
I hate you now,
Repeated
As the bells of love and hate
Bang, clang, sing
Like a record playing backwards.

Yet you want to love
With the full moon,

Where the rabbit lives,
Smiling magically
              Into your eyes.

So your brain
Sends you running,
Touching the corners of the room,
Hands pressing the spongy walls,
"Where are you rabbit,
I know you are real."
As the bruise like stains
Take the shape
              Of your palms.

Untitled

Look what you've done.
Spoken soft with tears.

Look what you've done.
Delivered with a force.

Look what you've done.
Delivered against a plea
      For understanding.

Please.
Stop shouting.

Unhappy ending

Is it hate
When you look at people
As if they have no sensitivity
Beyond their presence?

Is it hate
When you shout at them,
Frustrated in your protective zone,
Eyes closed to them.

You can be kind,
You can love, demanding it's fairy tale,
Denying it's happy ever after
In fear of missing an ending.

So you cut,
Severing the story, creating
An early ending of hate
Before love can save you.

That is control
Giving no desired finish,
An ending that blinds the need,
That need for a pause.

Dots.

The orange neon light of the petrol station
Spreads softness across the forecourt.
The dulled outline of castle on the hill
Contains a mountain of history,
But shades it with darkness.
Orange-blushed flesh against blue-green water
Are words that come to me for no reason,
But a poetic memory on some article read
Late in the night, as a sweaty mind
Minces with the law of simultaneous contrast.
All story tellers are thieves.

A gloved hand put them in my pocket,
Leaving no fingerprints. Although,
Your fingerprints are all over me.

The question comes inside, turns
And churns inside the smoke of a cigarette.
Foolish me, I thought I had stopped.
This is not a painting I am standing in.
But I can fool myself if so required.
Those dots, those blurs, centuries old,
Play tricks with the light.
If combining red and yellow over grey,
I will see orange over a neutral tone.
Until I apply the law. The grey

Will share with the eye,
A tint of orange. And,
The neutral grey will imply
A subtile blue where the colours meet.
The orange will stand out more powerful
In this ruse set against biased neutrality.

This is the scam of love and hate,
As the colours fight for control
Of abstract space they are brushed upon.
Without hate, the orange would not stand
                                So proud.
Much depends on how you look at it.
Much depends on what some creator
                                Wants you to see.
Much depends on who applies a law,
Where the mind plays with the palette,
And you see what you want to see.
You see sunflowers following the sunlight,
Closing in the night, tormented by the dream
Of transient love that triggers the rush of hormones
That trigger durable hate.

Dinner for two

I want to take you out for dinner,
My lover,
    My tormentor.
Just you and me.
We will leave the ragged boy with the gun,
The one held so tight against my temple,
As I kneeled for you and swallowed
Your kindness, and choked on your bark.
You, an officer and a gentleman,
Sighing at the ideals of love and hate,
Spinning them like full plates of offering
Balanced on bending canes, all
In some search for applause at your technique.

I would love to take you out to dinner,
With silver service and candlelight,
Drinking fine red wine and picking the bones
Of jugged hare softened in the stew, its sauce
Thickened by the creature's own blood.
And when the pudding comes,
I will pull the trigger of the gun,
Concealed under the table,

And make you jump as you ignite taste buds with
The bitterness of an unconventional lemon sorbet,
Served in a crystal glass dish,

                Lemon, with its own white pith.

The geranium kiss

I have experienced love
And hate.
And I have tasted the side dish,
Fragility.

It continues its invasion of comfort zones,
Here in the rambling, low-beamed country-cottage,
Home to all dreams of perfection,
Surrounded by thorny rose bushes that climb the walls,
Whose prick comes with the scent of a geranium kiss,
Carried on a summer breeze
Through the heart of love's open window.
Through the moth-eaten gossip gaps
Of hate's shady net curtains.
It brings that sour smell and bitter taste,
That plague the senses,
Nurtured in the place called home.

Hate, Love, Love, Hate,
Those melting polar poles of emotion,
Seeping and mixing within each other,
In that quaking, fragile world of molten core,
Of rock and soil, of sea and rivers,

Of subjective ugliness
>   And beauty.

Of flesh and blood.
All swirling in the manifest
Of worlds within worlds.

I have experienced Love
And Hate,
Held apart by the flesh and bone
Of Fragility,
As it bubbles in the blood stream,
Haemorrhaging,
Fouling fresh air.

Into the cottage garden it drifts,
The sorrow, the disease,
The violence and the greed,
Madness, always the madness,
Driving the envy. Fuelling the pain.
Pandora's lid has shifted geographies,
To grow new histories,
Leaving fragile hope behind.
Here comes the breeze to collect the kiss,
Guiding its invasion to our nostrils,

Overwhelming our tastebuds,
Blinding us with tears
And deafening our ears
To the sound of understanding,
Denying touch to our nerve endings.

It drifts around the cocktail party,
Within the murmurs of the piano room,
Where cello, and blues guitar,
Saxophone and vibrant bass
Mix with the voices of talking drums.

Here we slow-waltz the dance of circumstance.

Here Love's eyeballs connect
Across a crowded room,
Where Hate comes to dig a parting.
Tangled in Fragility's pathways,

We root like cacti to stubborn spots,
Where the Geranium kiss is snagged.

With Hope trapped inside some mythical box,
Nothing moves to the centre of the room,
To stand on that magic rug of forgiveness.

That is the place where fur-ball Faith was swept,
Left to collect old dust from under the carpet.

I have experienced love
And hate.
And I have tasted the side dish,
Fragility.
Then comes the snap called Blame.

These are the days my friend

I have ideals beyond my life,
And I leave it to you:
Judge me by my spirit,
Not my age.
For all the pain,
My spirit tries to stay strong.
But some days it weakens.
Some days it can't fight.
Some days I want to crawl
Under my bed and live
With scary monsters
Who threaten,
                  But never bite.
Then some days I am strong,
Immortally so,
Super hero in the sky.
I burn like the sun
Without the question why.
But then, some days,
I am simple and shy.

In between strong and weak,

When I know who I am,
What I am with my legacy,
Those are the days I cry,
Those fragile days
When pieces start to break.

"You said the other day, as we walked around the park, that you felt with age you were becoming unattractive. I hope you don't mind… but I wrote you a poem."

Unattractive?

No.

You are beautiful.

My eyes tell me so.

My ears confirm.

Your smile speaks of laughter.

Your eyes carry the spirit of the inquisitive.

Okay!

You talk a lot.

But your voice is of a bird

With an underlying hint of sexy gravel.

You carry the sceptre of determined independence.

Unattractive.
                No.

Watching

I watched you tonight
With admiration.
The way you played
With tied back hair
That brought new shapes
To your face.

I wanted to put my arm
Around you,
Gently guide you in
Closer, safer,
Into a place of silence,
In thanks to your animation.

My eye caught you
Drinking soda like a child,
Pinched cheeks bringing liquid
With a fizz to your tongue,
Cooling your throat,
After stirring ice cubes
With a straw.

In doing so I was hunting
For a rolling soft laugh
And a casual relax,
As you discovered
A welcome to this resting place.

Numbers

I see fitful soldiers sleeping
Warriors waking, waiting
For an early call.
But the soldiers keep on sleeping
On camp beds in the hospital.
I hear some stop snoring,
Choking the last gurgles of life.
I see the warriors writing
Last letters to their wives.
I see the dawn is breaking.
Red and orange rises over the hill.
Soon the remainders will be marching,
Bayonets fixed against their will.
But the cannons do not care
Who they are,
Brave or cowards,
Soldiers or warriors,
Just numbers there.

In case you fall

>I watched you with puzzled eyes
>As you pedal

Fast to the top of the hill.

>And then,
>Within a second split by an age,
>You took off,

Flying on a bike,

>To land, back wheel first,
>Without a spill, just a slight skid.
>And, I was there, hands waiting
>Just in case,
>Twisting my wrists to applaud.

>I watched you as a teenager,
>Smoking dope.
>Drinking under-age,
>Meeting girls who slowed down to be caught.
>Maybe a fight or scuffle.
>Did you think I never knew?
>But I could see it in your eyes.
>And, I was there, hands waiting,
>Just in case.

Just in case.

>I watched you as a man, eyes proud.
>Eyes watering.
>Thinking of your travels,
>From Kyiv to Shanghai
>And on to Aberdeen.
>To Kabul
>And home to Kyiv to volunteer.

I shivered with each bomb,
>Each bullet that flew,
>With each number,
>Each name of who dies.
>But I was there,
>Invisible.
>Hands waiting,
>Wringing.
>Just in case,

Just in case you fell.

Human?

He stood next to barbed wire,
His boyhood blue eyes, they must have earned him
Cheek pinches and smothering cuddles.
But the young soul was pierced.
His soul, prepared by dangerous words of hate:
"Those others are to blame." Fact.

I could have pinched those childish cheeks,
Lovingly calling you ugly
To protect you from the evil eye.
But the evil eye found you.
And your ears listened.
Your nose sniffed.
And your touch balled into a fist.
But I am human.
A dirty one to you.
A part of the mass,
The ones you need to kill.
Love is a distant memory
Packed in a box and put in storage.
Hate. Your mind turned
On the chemical swivel of biology.

Deep inside your mind,

That need to blame

For sins we, the others, aimed at you.

So you strip me naked.

You swallow viagra and rape me.

Punch and kick and waterboard me.

Your laughter is loud in my ears.

My scream is welcomed by your arms.

How could I hate you,

I could be you,

On the other side.

History

I have history ingrained inside of me,
Stored in the places where they mingle
                                    With today.
Memories cannot disappear
To please another. They must stay.
And with them the lessons learnt
From those days it went wrong.
Wrong, but never sour in the long term.
Around the table, where dreams dine,
Eat and drink together,
There is laughter,
                    Joy
                            And sweetness
Served in courses to remember.

These are not the cheese and wine
For your jealousies
That have slapped me.
Keep the album to look back upon,
One of songs and pictures,
Times that need to be treasured.
Without them I would not

Be here today

Next to you

In your restless sleep.

But can I stay with all these hurdles

You set before me.

I can leap them for a while

Until my body aches,

I grow tired,

Turn my back and sleep without peace.

Is love not a human trait,

And hate a traitor to yourself.

Am I the one with baggage.

Some yes, but why

Do you pick up the cases

And complain about their weight.

History's pages turn tomorrow.

"Love is wise, hatred is foolish," - Bertrand Russell. Friedrich Nietzsche asserted that both love and hatred are powerful forces that must be cultivated and understood. He could argue that a healthy individual, the so called superman, would not be afraid to hate something that is decadent, weak or life-denying. That in turn would perhaps make hate a creative, life-affirming force.

The Stoics, the likes of Seneca and Marcus Aurelius, supported Apatheia, freedom from passion. All passions, such as intense love or intense hatred, were irrational movements that disturbed inner peace. They argued that love and hate could, in their extreme forms lead to a loss of rational control. A wise person, in the eyes of the Stoics, would be guided by reason and virtue rather than fickle emotional swings. Detachment!

On the political scale, George Orwell sums up hate through O'Brien, the high ranking party member addressing Winston Smith. He says: "If you want a picture of the future, imagine a boot stamping on a human face - for ever." He goes on to say:" Do not forget that, Winston. The Party is not interested in power for its own sake. It is interested in power because it is power."

It is possible to scale this down, right down, into families, into the playground, where control and bullying can be seen. Hate has a selfish drive borne from insecurities, protection, blame, and probably abuse that has been handed down and passed over from one generation to another. We must not be weak, we must be strong, and that means domination. Yet those who hate can be very insecure.

Not everyone agrees that love and hate are polar to each other.

"The opposite of love is not hate, it is indifference, total absence of emotions. If you still hate someone, it means that you still care about that person." - Paulo Coelho, The Devil and Miss Prym. Others have said apathy is more in opposition to Love than hate. But is it not that case that the "I don't care…" attitude is one of hate's many pillars. For example, to say I don't care" equals the sending of a hate message.

The undeniable pulse

Is it real to think that love's warmth
Tightens our chest and holds a sweet embrace.
Or hate, fills us with shadows that we can chase.
Put every gentle thought to a test
To discover when gentleness shatters.
But the core question matters:
Do love and hate overlap
In strange non-fiction,
                        Bubbling in some convenient guise.
Is truth reflected in a lover's eyes,
The quiet comfort, shared without a sound,
Where true connection can be deeply found.
Look now to where shadows often creep,
Where words can sow what the angry reap.
Airborne tension, sharp rejection, sudden fury,
Prejudice, all found in dark corners.
Love and Hate, polar forces shaking dice
For worldly games, big worlds, small worlds,
Games that give and take without measure.
Rolling snake eyes can make hearts leap
Into the crucible of cherished love and the hates we keep.
Are these not the fabric of the human soul,

Making us fractured, making us whole.
Stirred primal forces seek to define
What cannot be defined.

The unsteady edges of now

Love is for grasping all that we hold so dear,
As tailored beings spin it from the air,
And build it on what is convenient and near.
It is built to tumbling point.
One that snuggles into a small picture.
Grows into a bigger picture
And crashes into insignificance
As the picture grows anaemic on thinning canvas.

The white areas are painted smooth,
But then draw the shadows in.
The picture emerging in colours soft and deep,
A gentle hand, a promise it will keep.
But, from within the skin of paint, a figure
Disguises a bruising touch, a whisper turning cold,
A hate, burning bright,
Devouring reason in its hungry light.

The ending of love.
The ending of hate.
Both mark us until we die.
Reality pockets love's embrace,

And hate's whispered sigh.
Love and hate know the ghost
Of their own end.

Standing under a mellow street lamp

There a man in a trilby,
It's brim filling with rainwater.
His raincoat collar turned up,
Damp patches on his shoulders.
Two eyes, scissor-cut into his newspaper,
Are closing as they turn to papier-mâché.
A silent world, or so it seems,
Measured by the light that screens,
He thinks, from another's view.
His subjective lens, shapes the damp,
The grey,
      The blue.
The newsprint bleeds, a truth defined,
By what the eye and what the mind
Tries to gauge from what is seen,
Through a quantum blur of jealousy.

Even as the streetlamp glows,
Reality shifts, as the river flows.

Ephesians 4:26-27 (NIV):

"In your anger do not sin": Do not let the sun go down while you are still angry, and do not give the devil a foothold."

Unexpected Hell

A thunderstorm flash.
A banging bolted door.
Rain, cold, with acid drops.
Words from a shotgun mouth
Explode to open-up the chest,
Exposing the one organ
That holds love in its rhythm
And hate in the momentary pause
Between each beat.

The breath comes quick,
The vision blurs,
As tempest in the mind occurs,
Spurred by the well-oiled click
Of a trigger pulled by a well-aimed finger
That, having opened the wound,
Pokes the wound, and explores
With a poisoned rage that takes its toll,
Leaving its scars on a frozen soul.

The reflected glow of Hell's burning lake
Shivers orange and blue in each fearful eye,
Longing for that odourless life of pure sulphur.
Let the prosaic and banal circle like wagons,
Stopping to give protective space
Between the axles and wheels of rough movement.

Stop shouting, stop shouting, stop shouting
But even when it stops, its echo hovers
In the stink of burnt matches

And yet, despite this heat of fire and fry,
Look. It is a cold, frozen-over place.
Unexpected hell, full of sighs with no relief.
Waiting is part of the game, looking for that moment,
When all will turn to love and normal once again.
From this, underground footsteps fade to decay,
As they climb towards some light of day.
Dreaming of how it might have been, but knowing
It feels impossible to stay.

Once frozen out, spin to find yourself
Frozen in, within an even colder place.
The outside world has drained and drifted far away,
Leaving you as a ghost, unseen, unheard,
Haunted by every harsh, cruel flung word.
Inside this void, where dreams die and fade,
A desolate, cold world was made.
Tremors start inside a hollow chest,
Whispering a cry for peace,
                    For rest.

Shooting star

I saw a shooting star last night,
And first, I thought of you.
Then I thought
It is just space hardware,
Zipping through the cosmos,
                                  Somewhere.
Then I thought it was a missile
Flying overhead,
Heading with a flaring tail
To wake the child in her bed.
Or to kill the one I love the most,
And send her off to see some holy ghost.
I saw a shooting star last night.
I think it was you.

Untitled

Bitter shame, silent chill, Fear and uncertainty
Start to spill blood red petals across the cage floor,
And blood follows,
As the heart beats fast, like a frantic, trapped bird's wing.
The air punctures self-esteem, again you think
What might have been, and what? Hold on, hold on tight,
You say it inside your head in some imagined fight.
"Get out of my life," "I wish you dead," The words start to sing.
As they cruelly apply their most venomous sting.

Framing the tempest

Headless,
Heedless of the crush of pain,
Hand holding head under the flow
As the crimson tide runs through a vein.
As the right to anger is fully claimed
Through heart and mind, the tempest is framed.

From where
Does it spring, this simmering blame,
Whose volcanic eruption sours the air, with claim
Of some injustice repeated time, and time again.
Eyes deepened in a headlight stare,
A dragon's hulking shadow dances
On the wall,
 Across the ceiling,
A bouncing sound trapped in closed space,
A primal scream finds no place to hide,
Until it has pierced a brain with an icicle spear
Of fire, as nostrils flare, stomping feet
Crush all around, without a care.

Historic sins,
Spin inside the brain, having cracked

That tough skin of bone-hard plate,
Cutting into that tender spot that once inspired love,
Turning it lathe-like into unforgiving hate,
Justifying that need to scream, to shout.

Pause.
Please.

The rabbit

The rabbit,
The one that lives in the moon,
Shivers unseen, Praying to the sun
It will be over soon, so it can run
To the darkness of its room,
And fight stinging traumas,

     As the moon-nettles bloom.

The vibration of love and hate

Deep connection,
Linked by deeper emotion.
So, the door is open.
Vulnerable shadows pass in and out,
Fearing the light will snuff itself.

The more love, the more to lose
As, like lovers do, they entwine
With each others actions,
With feelings. And we wait.
Time passes with anxious expectation.

The heart string plays its tune,
Finger-plucked by the paradox
Of that thin line taught and tuned
To bend the ballroom notes
Of love, of hate, and lament.

That hanging note,
The deep throated note,
That cuts the juke joint's
Smoke filled air,
Where planks bounce
And dust dances,
A fire where wood turns to coals
That blow and glow.

And as the mind wanders,
Distorted perception feeds
Off the love and into
The ugly mouth of hate.
And the energy of the eyes
Turns to the energy of the fist,
That turns into a shout,
A scream for lost love.

Door shuts and shadows fade
In the coolness of the dawn.
It will never happen again,
Sorry, so sorry. The sorry,
Always repeated.

Hope looks in the mirror on the wall
And utters the words of fairy tales.
Nothing changes without time.
With time, those furrows of pain,
They get deeper.

Argument

Always on guard
Against the traumas of the past.
Each shout nails home lowly self esteem.
It pins it to the floor, to the out-of-reach ceiling.
As the shout's pitch shatters glass.

Deeply embedded,
Deeper than the bed of love,
Lay the breathing corpse of
The shame and worthlessness
Of loves undeserving guilt.

Each tries to own the blame.
Each prays for a forgiveness
That never comes. Never
Crosses the floor,
But in stillness, builds walls
For protection against the next shout,
The next fist, leaving a hollow stranger
Who looks familiar.

True Love versus Love

Love lives in the tension
of the water's surface,
Rising with the waves of lust.
Infatuation's thrill lifts and falls
As the hand reaches for connection
To bring a dream to life.

Romantic love, now this is desire,
The boat that will carry two souls
To some desert island,
Some shared isolation of sun and sand.
For those blind to the passing ships.

But true love is for those who dive deep,
Sharing the air from the tanks they carry.
They understand the need to breath.
With respect and trust, they pass the mouthpiece,
And inhale to stay strong for each other.

Together they invest in a submarine,
To escape the killer whales that surround them.
Modest in expense, rich in satisfaction.
They read the same books of pirates

Who raided the South China Seas

And share the tales over cups of tea,
Before waving with a see-you-later smile,
As one goes fishing for minnows,
And the other to fight with salmon,
Not caring who gets more.

True lovers do not play in the Octopus's garden.
They help plant it and watch it grow.

Deep in the water, time moves
To different currents where
The laughter of air bubbles make pleasing sounds.
On the crowded surface of the seas.
Snorkel-lovers watch those few below.
Through their perspex goggles,
They laugh at boring lives.

Those below,
        Deeper,
                Only glance in return.

Simple

You are tired.
Lay your head softly
On my shoulder and sleep.

I have space for you there.

I will sit still
In soft yellow candle light,
Breathing to your rhythm
and
My eyes will watch
The shadow of a flame
Dance across your dreams.

I have time for you there.

Gambling on a broken heart

Love each other,
Or not,
And we know where that may lead.
The heart beats either way,
Rotating inside,
A twisted dynamic heart
That spews forth rainbow petals
Or spiral pointed thorns.
Both come from the same branch,
Or sprig, or stalk.
And stalk they will,
To impress some position
That will say love
        Or hate,
As if choice really came into it.
They spin, slow and stop
Like some gamblers roulette wheel.
As we know, such wheels cannot be trusted.
For artful disguise tries to win a heart,
Trick a heart, to confuse or play hard to get.
Much lays in the motive to gamble.

The big picture

Is it time to look at the big picture.
Impossible.

It is so big.
I cannot see it all in one go.

Hard as I try.
My senses must move around it.

Like seeing Guernica
For the first time.

I had to move around,
Inside and outside at different angles.

What I had seen,
I saw again, but differently.

Just seeing was not enough.
It never is. You need the touch, the smell, the sound.

You need the love.
And the hate. And the joy. And the fear.

You need expectation.

So, fall into the big picture.
Immediately you are lost. No lighthouse to guide you home.

But keep moving,
Away from the dogs that follow in the distance.

You must find it,
That key that holds the big picture together.

Go back to the little pictures.
Look hard for the common ground.

          Start digging.

    Without little pictures
    No big ones can grow.

I cannot die

He spoke Russian with his enemy,
Saying, I cannot die in this war.

Only if you forget my eyes
Will I die,
Only if my smile, my songs,
My music and my love,
Is forgotten by those who love me,
Will I die.

My wife,
My children, brother, sister, friends,
They will blend my laughter with theirs.
And tears will join in a babbling stream
Where fishes, the keepers of dreams,
Swim.

And his enemy said:
Then I will not kill you,
In a different world
We could have been friends.
Maybe we will both meet soon.
In a different world.

As he spoke, he pushed and pressed
His bayonet home.

And, as his enemy lay bleeding against him,
In his arms,
A bullet from the sheltering trees
Entered his brain,
Leaving no time for words,
But instantly creating a new time
For a meeting, with a new friend.

And far away, a small town stands broken.
Crushed more by a missile in the sky.
It is there where wives, children, sisters,
                Brothers and friends died.
And, upside down in the aftershock,
                        Fish float.

Looking for a friend

As an old man walked from the dust cloud,
His back arched and knapsack light,
A kind face asked a question:
"Who died today?"
The old man looked at the stranger's eyes,
Saw them brim with tears, as he replied:
"I don't know, I never knew them.
"I am only here by chance."

And the kind stranger thanked the old man,
Saying: " I was hoping you could help me find a friend."

A Kyiv girl (Avdiivka has fallen)

Trying to be brave,
To be polite,
The Kyiv girl with a smile
Hides her pain.

She spoke with a final tremor
Out of time with her shaking hand.
A telegram with bad news flutters
With death on the front line.

Avdiivka,
A city born from nomads,
Then heaving with industry,
Then piled with rubble,
A roof,
For those living underground.

Married, she may have lived there,
One day raised children, maybe.
It was then the siren sounded.
She walked unsteadily toward the shelter.
She fell into step with the shudder around her.
It's rhythmic suck stealing her air.

She stopped.
Began to stare.
Even in death
She could not stop looking.
A sigh.
> A relief.

Her war over.
Her lover's too.
Her telegram catches a breeze...

The road to Freetown (Sierra Leone) "Operation No Living Thing"

I bought cigarettes, rough tasting cigarettes,
From her small shop on the road to Freetown.
She had no arms.
She had no legs.
Just stumps.
She had children and a smile.

Then that sad, sick : "Operation No Living Thing"
Set invulnerable savagery a-light, eyes bright, clothes
Tattered and torn and sandals worn, but the devils were dancing.
With insect bites and bitterness, with guns and grenades,
The soldiers of hate arrived on her doorstep, looking down
On Freetown.

Her smile was born from survival.
She says God is true.
Near where her shop now stands,
She was left in the road.
String and cardboard, hanging around her neck,
Delivering a message. A warning
To anyone daring to oppose
The superboy rebels.
She was repeatedly raped.

She was cut.

She was chopped.

Left in the road,

Expected to die

Amidst the damp fragrance of greenery,

The Lipstick Plant.

    The white flagged Peace Lilies,

The Cardboard Plant,

A remnant from the time of dinosaurs.

The tropical flowers,

Ancient growth that added blood to history,

They heard her, heard her prayer, and

From dew drop to dew drip,

From petal to leaf,

From stem to the earth,

Her voice passed to the worms.

And from petal to bee,

And,

A miracle took place.

She survived.

But her plea for a better world

Remains suspended on a cross.

Gaza

The apartment building where I lived,
Well, part of me still does,
                          Is quite beautiful.
In its own way of course.
Beauty is, as you know,
Eye of the beholder.
Six stories high, as I
Stand at the bottom and
Look up to the top,
To the place called home.

I see blue sky and clouds
Floating beyond the reality of where I live.
When I stood on one of three balconies
I could still not touch those clouds,
Or add paint to that sky,
Constant in its out of reach domain.

Then,
The top of the building
Embraced the ground,
Smothering it with surprise.
Such meeting was unexpected.

Oh dear,
Everything has moved.
Gone into the past tense.

I would have invited you for tea
But it is unlikely you can come.

The magical street

Once I lived in a magical street
Where kids kicked tin cans,
Knocked on doors and ran,
Or stayed for a biscuit
Or some other treat.

Such is the joy of a terraced house,
In the middle of a terraced street.

My neighbour was English,
The other was Welsh.
Then there were the Asian families
From India,
From Pakistan, and Bangladesh.

And all the kids were snot encrusted
With smiles and trust and fights,
Sharing the spoils of shoplifting
But never in the corner shop.
There they got sweets for free,
And their mums and dads had credit.

And the Caribbean couples

Who laughed on their doorsteps,
Whose windows opened
To release a glorious, sweet smell
That tempted the Turkish barber,
So much so, that he adopted dreadlocks.

And the smells of cooking wafted
Down the street and up our noses.
As we shared the dishes of
Bhuna, Yorkshire puddings,
Jerk chicken and pepper-pot stew.
Rare bites of bara broth and cawl,
All inviting the tastebuds
Of Six Dinner Syds
Who made well-timed calls.

On Fridays and Sundays
We were all well fed.
When the Chinese moved in
Spring rolls came too,
And the Syrian refugees
Brought waraq 'inab
And laughed with the Turks
At the different names for dolma,

Comparing tastes.

Walking home from The Queen Vic,
Bemoaning those colonial days,
We danced clumsy steps to the music
Beaten out on dustbin lids,
The well-pitched mbira,
The rhythm of the oud
And the baglama.
With the talking drum,
The guitar strummed along.

The magical street where
The words of world poets
Echoed from the minds and memories
Of unforgotten homelands.
Darwish, Hikmet traded verse.
Putuma, Seth and Wang Wei,
Hughes and Dylan,
All got a mentions too.

And here,
In the magical street,
We found freedom
In a trapped place.

And I laughed
When my father took me aside
During a Sunday dinner,
Where, he insisted on a spoon
As I ate with my fingers.
He said:
"You'll never sell this house."

Ten seconds later, That laugh,
My laugh, to his distaste,
Echoed down the street.

The politics of the night

The silent flight of the owl,
The stalking step of the pussycat,
Hard to see,
Hard to hear,
They are quietly out preying
In force tonight.

Pooh, piss and plumage mark
Their borders.

And,
If those borders cross
They may fight, or
Eat each other.
But,
Before such a strike
A risk check is made.
A blink of an eye,
A frozen pause,
Weighing up
The power of their claws.

Spare a thought

For the territorial mouse,
Whose regular track weaves
Around the lands claimed
By owls and cats,
And probably others too:
The weasel, the stoat,
The runaway ferret,
Their names define them.

There is the humbug badger
With his diet of worms,
He sniffs for flesh and fruit,
He lives in a clan, but
Keeps to himself, not willing
To share his treasure of
Bulbs and birds' eggs.

And then of course,
The ginger coated fox,
Whose fur goes dull
When he strays too long
On the wrong side of the border,
To raid the lands,
Creeping, darting, undercover,

From dustbins to chicken coup,
He slyly goes,
In commando-manoeuvres.

And there they stand,
Fighting cocks in hand,
The worst of enemies,
Whose borders are marked by
Barbed wire, wood and hedges,
Even a well-drawn line
Marks mother-nature's back.
And they protect it with weapons
Of mass-destruction, a fiery barrel,
A snarling dog, trained to betray
Nature's calling, and,
Of course,
      A spray of poison.
They are the mother's wunderkind.

Keep that thought though,
For the omnivorous mouse,
Who chooses a diet of seed,
Fruit and nuts, whose shells
He can crack.

As he scurries the food-trail.
He will cross the borders,
He will pay the price.
He may scare a lion
And take his roar,
Or even send shivers of fear
To a farmer's wife.
He may breed like a rabbit
                            But
He only desires an ordinary life
Outside the politics of the night.

Ten seconds later,
An owl ate him.

The golden tree

Who can think without horror
What another war could mean?
Yet think we do, and,
We still go to war
And inflict its manifold misery.

So I think instead
Of the Golden Rain Tree,
With its spread of branches,
Its soft toothed leaves
And yellow four-petalled flowers.

They can help divide our gardens
And create a calm serenity
As indoors we see the footage
Of buildings crushed to dust,
Of refugees who walk a long way
                    From me.

Their homes, their gardens,
Their schools and libraries,
Museums of ancient culture,
Lay in ruins, but, sipping tea
I look out at the long garden.

It's neatness continues to amaze,
Kept so by a Syrian gardener
And his love for flowers,
And his longing for trees in
A peaceful landscape.

He arrives by bus,
And today planted the Tree of Heaven
With its large leaves with elliptical leaflets.
And he will break the lines he plants
With Northern Japanese Magnolia.

All these trees are new to him,
With his memories wrapped around
The craggy Olive that matches his taste.
I watch him kneel to face Mecca,
Praying for what by me is not known.

But I sense a longing, for a chance
To take these orderly trees of colour
And durability, to plant them at home.

He leaves by bus, but knows for sure
The place he is going to, is not home.

Only he knows

Checking in the broken mirror,
He sees his smile disguised depression
Remains in place.

He whistles a folk song to make an acceptance
Within himself.

And the sky listens. It turns into "a moonlit, starry,
Clear night."

His feet, wrapped in holy socks and second hand bandages,
Get stuffed into two worn boots.

He is waiting, with an exhalation of breathy mist,
For expectant slush and mud to seep through unlaced eyelets.

He stands inside his head, looking for the stories,
The nightmares and noises.

They belong to him, part of him, loved by him.
They are him and his.

Which side are you on

The protest songs,
For spirited youth to imagine peace
Wearing Woodstock flowers in their hair.

Sample the apple pie at Alice's.
To stave off hunger's hole,
To talk it through with guitars strumming,
To be honest and say: we don't want to die.

But who can listen or think as
The drums thump strong and
The bugles blow loud
To drown out the sound of objection.

And who can listen, who can think
As guitar notes bend a warning call,
To arms, to arms, link arms
And have the courage to fall
Into Forseti's strong arms,
Under the banner of right and wrong.
But pray Baldr is your true father
But even justice and forgiveness can fool you.
Soldier Blue and magic mushroom mumblers,
Marching to different drums,
Fight the false god Moloch inside you

Let him not stand in front of God.

And spare thoughts for the innocent,
Those who live on the Earth,
But do not wage war as the world does,
Controlling everything in a spin.

But we must wait, and wait some more.
One man can change in Winter
As he discovers his own invincible summer.
But can we do it all together?

Wait and wait some more, can you?
For as the mass graves, mass rapes,
Left over mines and radiation gathers,
We must wait for the power of love,
And pray it overwhelms
The love of power. Or join
Those brave heroes of history,
The fallen 300.

The success of both sides
Is only temporary.

John Barleycorn is dead

Private John Barleycorn's breath disappears,
Along with the other clouds of bad breath.
His defiant cries have turned to ice.
Those repetitive cries that no longer scare
The silent ones sitting under leaf-strewn nets,
Sharpening scythes to cut away legs.
We do not see who is there,
Not even the whites of eyes,
These are the unknown ones from unknown places.

Their slicing cuts make Barleycorn bleed,
To end the misery of waiting, please, strike.
And strike they do, to honour their vow
That John Barleycorn must die.
Just as curious, blinded, earless heads
Turn to see who stands and who falls.
And others stand and fall, stand and fall,
These little picture scenes,
Scenes filling a storm blown cornfield,
Husks dust the air, leg-stems fall and fall
For all to see. Or not. As the case may be.

Death has, in that lingering second that follows life,
Walked into the golden field. And, as arms swing,
We linger in that ecstasy of an ending.
A silence for survivors, a silence trapped,
Inside and behind wide eyes and ringing ears.
A head twisting, ringing ten decibels above the norm.
The half-dead slowly stand, one-by-one,
Bent with acid churning guts, retching.
Buzzing in the left ear sounds a warning.

The mincing machines are following.
Orthodox crosses borrowed from the dead,
Are touched. Prying fingers explore
A tortured soul's wound.
He hangs pinned. Tongue swollen.
Mother weeping. Pitchfork wielders,
Crab stick threshers, and worse,
The miller grinds John Barleycorn
Between two large stones.

The crows, The odd raven, and
The thieving magpies circle in the air.
They gather in the trees to greedily stare
At charred flesh, blood and crushed bones,
Checking Private Barleycorn is dead.

For he, and others, are the carrion
They will harvest.

Who knows, Wheat may grow here one day,
One blue summer season. Maybe beet for borscht.
Food feeds those thoughts of a harvested life,
One few will taste, or want to taste,
Because
      They know.
Know why

                      The black earth is rich.

Peace may come John Barleycorn
And you will be called hero, martyr.
Or some other name given to the lost.
But those who live on will remember;
John Barleycorn is dead.
They will raise toasts to you
With brandy in a nut-brown bowl.
Or vodka, or ale to wash down
That solemn prayer.

And the seeds
Your blood and bones helped grow,
Will be swallowed.

"We yield thee hearty thanks and praise for the return of seedtime and harvest, the increase of the ground and the gathering of the fruits, and for all the other blessings of thy merciful providence bestowed upon this nation and people." - Book of Common Prayer, 1979 Protestant Episcopal Church, United States.

Another trap door

The condemned generals and commanders
Stood erect and still in a perfect line.

Medals on their chests looked dull.

Breathing steadily, they wait for the rope,
The drop.

Under his breath, under the hood,
He whispered: " I am sorry for you."

"Then you should walk free now, " came the reply.
"You lack true evil."

This secret whisper remained unheard,
Drowned by the sound just before death,

Just before the final kicks and wet-fronted trousers.
The walls of pride vanquished.

Blurred

We have the white magic.
Love can send a voice
Out into space,
Leaving it to be discovered
By those who want to find it.
Then love can be returned.

We have the black magic.
Hate can weaponise a satellite,
Create a fear that one day
A red button will be pressed
By an ordered finger,
Turning hate against hate returned.

Once installations complete,
All is so simple.
Love and hate.
Life and death.
Orbiting around us
With smiles and frowns.

Inside photographs from space
We can see Earth, our little earth

Where we spin and stand still.
Its colours show us place
And the vastness that surrounds it,
A huge crowded emptiness.

We are no more than a pinhead
When looked at from without.
We are a chaotic dance
When viewed from within.
We are the tiniest of a time capsule,
Storing love and hate.

Watched through glass,
Cells stirring inside
Our rolling laboratory's petri dish.
But the culture cannot see out.
Blind eyes locked into little pictures,
Missing the breath that holds us
        Inside the big picture,
                The vast picture

It is the picture that holds all existence
Alongside our existence,
Which it cups in the hand of time and space,

Glues it with gravity, and
Inside the dance of selfish simplicity and limit,
Our transcendence is kept at bay.

We miss the big picture that sits
Deep within the even bigger picture.

The Bunker with a magic door

The jangle of keys hanging
                          On an overcrowded ring.
None would fit.
The sliding credit card,
The bent hair grip.
Neither did the trick.
So I stood back,
        Remembered the magic words of childhood.
        Remembered life is but a dream.
        Eyes closed and still.
I watched.
The ironmonger key,
Old, cold and large,
Float into the pawn shaped hole.
And twists.
The heavy clicks and squeaky hinge.
The sticking door opened with a shove.
There I saw a child who called me.
"Follow", I said, "You have forgotten too much."

Umbrellas

This land of umbrellas
Wielded with wilfulness
As shields against the sun.

Until, that is, the limited shade
Is overtaken by a payload
Locked like black death

Deep inside swelling
Grey trimmed clouds,
Edged in silver.

Locks tumble, rain drops
Like sheets unfolding.
The rising downpour forces
Thin, lanky Umbrella legs to twist
And people to run from being
To being blown inside out.

Idi Amin: "You have freedom of speech. But freedom after speech, that I cannot guarantee."

So,
What is the question.
The question is what is the question?
Well, if that is a question,
This is the answer.

But what if the answer is wrong,
Unacceptable,
Deniable,
Not what you want to hear.

Then this is an argument
Where sight of the answer
Will be lost.

And perhaps
There is more than one answer.
Nothing strange about that.
So, find your answer to suit.

Then you can wear the answer
With some pride of discovery.

But those who disagree,
Will chalk a sign or sew a patch
Upon your sleeve,
Or lapel,
Or breast.

And you will be the walking answer.
Displayed like a peacock,
Making their answer
Unequivocal.

You know,
It is easy to tweak a question.
And there you are, trapped
Without an answer.

You can, of course, ask questions,
You have freedom of speech.

To Andrew Marvell

My thoughts?
They churn in the current of her gentle art,
That keeps me yearning with a guarded heart.
So in this heat of desire and denied passion,
I am frozen.

Cold stillness keeps me strong
But my fear of the fragility it guards
Keeps my vegetable love secure
In the ground where its seed is also buried.

Muse

I watched you last night
With the intensity of a painter
Staring at his naked muse,
Wondering how to colour you on canvass.

I looked, no, stared directly
At your eyes coated in mussel shells,
Dark and layered on the outside,
Until, in a flash of laughter, they sparkled.

Flashes timed in hip-hop moves
From unhappy arguments
To medical problems that inflict
Women of a maturing age.

Then the shrug.
Then the smile.
Then the laugh.
Then the sigh.

My cubic eyes orbited yours,
Each angle glimpsed in one.
Each point of light stirred acuity

With sharp keenness to understand.

But I did not need to understand.
I just needed my eyes to talk to you,
Saying in whispers that I am here.
I whispered: I am here.

Home

The map tattooed on his body was etched
In invisible scars,
Scars that were always just one step away
From being traced
By confused thoughts, directions
and spinning symbols
Lost in the miasma of decay.

But his body was home now,
Wearing the clothes stored
And ironed for the homecoming.
Clothes that now hung loose
With an extra notch in the belt,
Looped into folds of the unfit.

Loved ones welcomed him.
He had been missed, worried about.
How his smile broadened at the greeting point,
As he slid from the discomfort of a flatbed truck.
But that smile, with that lingering bodily fetor,
Was fighting for the place in his eyes.

His face was harrowed,

His spirit ploughed. His face.
Each crease and line and blackhead
Lay deep, rough like a sludge bogged ditch
Beneath thorn hedges that ripped uniforms,
Impossible to repair..

Now he was home. Waiting.
Waiting for the assembly lines to roll,
The hiss of the air hose, the tightening of a nut.
The boredom of normality,
The sigh of safety.

When he looked at her,
Fussing over guests at his welcoming party,
Being polite to the elderly, kind to the cousins,
Arguing with a sister about the table setting,
Sending kids to bounce on the marital bed,
A thought deepened the sockets of his eyes:
There is no sense and love is meaningless.

Borders

On the other side of the wrought iron fence,
Nakedness is frowned upon.
Apples make us wary of evil snakes that talk.
But the lesson has never been learned,
Or seen.
We never left the Garden of Eden.

Instead, we fenced ourselves inside,
Building our barriers to its technical purity.
Building our barriers to its immortal demands.
Building our shelters against the eyes of God,
                            The guilt of creating
And the moral code created.

For how could we leave a space that never,
Not really, had a gate that kept us out of reality.
Out of reality's harmful temptations, unless
We were the gate, hinged with creaks and crimes.
Hinged with the sins of temptations to live
Unclean lives.

But the fancy fences, the stone walls,

That gave us shade, shelter and protection
Were always in danger of holes and seepage
Caused by the weakness of earth,
The flow of rivers and the shaking in the ground.

The modular protection system,
Made from steel plates with internal support,
And filled with sand. We called it modern.
We called it technology to defend
Our defences from dents, scrapes,
Scratches and chips. Surrounded
By the parapet fortifications, a wall,
A trench deeper, a wall higher, thicker,
Crenellated.

They kept us in from perfection,
Protected immoralities from purities.
And so we grew in damage, betrayal.
A space for dishonesty where only the most honourable men
Could pose as honourable men.

Bon Voyage

Love can be seen as fundamental to life. It can also be seen as an irrational part of it. It does have an unpredictable nature. The French call this unpredictability - a love at first sight, for example - "le coup de foundre". Literally, it translates as "the thunderbolt".

Love, looked at from this perspective, can bring intense joy. When it sours, if it sours, then that elation turns to pain that can also bring intensity. But as Blaise Pascal said: "Love has its reasons that reason does not know." In other words, the irrational nature of love can easily twist the heart into its opposite: hate.

Serge Gainsbourg said: "Life is not worth living without love." He may have explored the scandalous side of love, the classic being his song with Jane Birkin, Je t'aime… moi non plus. Gainsbourg is linked with the sexual nature of love, which may be unfair. Of course its part is high significance, but love is not about the act, but the sensual spirit of the act. He also saw unconsummated love as most powerful.

Superstar Gainsbourg had a provocative persona, certainly colourful. But he, along with others, does make me question whether soulmate love truly exists, or whether it is about individual hormonal desires,

Tolerate and accept that if we have love, we will have hate, which in French eyes, may be strong, but not as strong as love. The French keep a perspective. Take this quote from a postcard: One can do a lot with hate, but even more with love. In French, it reads: On peut faire beaucoup avec la haine, mais encore plus avec l'amour. In French you can write with body language.

Part 1

Love is the art of failed storytellers.
It opens with bright eyes,
But as it turns. it's candle flickers,
Dying In melted wax.
And the story is what it is.
It can end in a drowning.
A hanging.
Or a sleep in the sawdust.
Or a looking up at the stars
From the gutter you lay in.

Take the risk love offers.
Say I love you with all the meaning that can be mustered.
See what happens.
Be true in what you say, what you believe.
Then love will stay for as long as you desire.
Until that split second,
That moment time steps in and says farewell.
With a pop.

Look out for it.
Shed a tear as needed,
Before you say bon voyage.
Bon Voyage Love.
"I will see you again when the time is right."

Part 2

I can fall in love.
Some say I can fall in love too easily,
But no. No.
That is not true.
I am not a highly sensitive dog
Sniffing out love and reacting
In a run-a-round sort of way.
Tail wagging.

I am more a man with a T-shaped vacuum nose.
Inhaling love's passionate beginnings.
Sense the air, feel the rhythms and
Yes, set eyes on the aurora.
Those sky-arcing colours,
All filling up the senses with awe
And wonder.

Love lives above all, so the imagination says,
A notion repeated in the books of love.
And loss.
It follows the pattern of change:
Storming in passion.
Forming in habit.
Norming in daily routine.
It sits high in the emotional rainbows.

Highly fragile. Sensitive. Like a bubble.
It is a party balloon bobbing around the room.
Until time wearies it,
And the invisible pin shimmers in the background.
And pops it.
Love has gone,
Not in any colourful, fading way,
But gone.

But when exactly was it the balloon popped?
That moment love turns to shrivelled, wrinkled rubber.

Enjoy the moment of love, but know
The wham-bam of sex wanes like the moon.
It turns to sensitive touch,
Before the touch becomes more gentle,
So feather-light it cannot be felt.

There, the high art of warped tragedy.

Treat it for what it is, say the counsellors in the bar.

Perhaps a burning at the stake.

Perhaps a flurry of perfumed petals
Lost in the wind of Geranium kisses.

Part 3

I can fall in love.
Some say I can fall in love too easily.
I can also say: Fare thee well to you,
You the one who once was my true love.

When life steps in wearing ballet slippers,
Do not fear or shy away.
Just be prepared to leap and lift,
But moreover, enjoy the dance
And fly like Peter Pan
After Wendy sewed his shadow on.
Be happy until time moves you on.
For it will, one way or another.
And the signs of it coming will be there.

Your drama teacher will pass by your room,
Step in with a flounce and, arm raised, will instruct:
Grow like a tree, reach for the sky, be strong.
You will start to unwind upwards,
And she will smile and bend around you.
Until the light changes to gloom,
To darkness, to a flash of lighting
That hides a sudden slice of movement.

Her knife will cut you.
Your sap will bleed out,
Be collected in a jar
Added to the shelf marked Past Love.

You may ask what have you done to deserve this.
Maybe ask what did I do to you to deserve this.
Perhaps just curl up into a ball and let storms rage.

Bitterness? It is all part of what we do,
Drama, darling, drama, the great disguise.
It is our armour against fear of exposure.
In another love, it could be your turn
To be the drama teacher.

Oh, before I forget:
if you kiss my one time love,
Just know It is okay.
Be happy until time moves you on.
For it will, one way or another,
And as the curtain falls, know:

A drink will be waiting on the bar for you.
Bon voyage.

The joint birthday party

What happens when the mother of the boy and the father of the girl meet in a crowded space.

Running ahead of parents,
Through closing iron gates to greet
Friends, cousins, delivering gifts
To the boy, the girl who share a birthday.

Hand-holding children run in rings
Of laughter and spins, songs that skip
Off the tongue, hide and seek, training
In that game of life and love has begun.

Following, in disappointed footsteps
With moans, groans, and squabbles,
Come the scorned and teased, and,
The angry losers at pass the parcel.

Until, with a pop of plastic flowers,
White birds ,and scared rabbits,
The magician arrives to open eyes
Wide with amazements; and to heal
The petty fractures of argument,
Re-settling the love in sunshine
And a measurement of sugar,

That sweetener before the break.

The man of magic weaves spells
And checks for satisfied customers.
He catches all others cannot see,
The Queen of Hearts is pulled
From the thinnest of air, She winks,
And the Knave and the Joker
Stir potions in the teapot,
Readying it to be served.

Circled around the heads of roar,
laughter, giggles and pushes, and
Dashes to the loo, parents chatter,
Sit at tables drinking tea, mulling
and milling over who is who and
the what, where, when and why's
Of daily life, sour and sweet.
In conversing shadows,
      Eyes meet.

The crowd blurs with embarrassment,
Someone might see the signs.
The quick glance, the smile hello,
The memory of a promise that means all.

That promise lingers, the one that says
Move on from love, move to true love
And share all, give all, be all for one.
As the magician pulls out his wand
                            And waves a hankie.

But the ones that make the signs,
The mother of the boy,
The father of the girl,
Know how to read the signs,
Know what the signs mean for them.
It stirs the feeling that makes Woland grin.

Hate fuelled by Azazello is stirred,
As bleak rejection digs deeper
Behind the eyes and the senses
Of watchers who cannot accept.
And, as he twists his knife of despair,
Margarita holds the lovers' hands,
And, with queen-like manner, takes them
Through hell and out the back door.

Omniscient in knowledge of love and hate,
Woland knows where the back door leads,
As he turns the daughter and son cards of guilt,

Adding gluttonous cream to the birthday cake.

The meowing magician's latest trick: the candles,
Lifted from Woland's secret store and
Fed by Hell fire, cannot be blown out.
He waits for Margarita to plead her case.

"Off with their heads", the Queen roars.
As she spins across the ceiling in a room
Where thinly disguised broken hearts weep,
And couples ponder their own sharp guilts.
Woland ponders a headless corpse.
And utters dear Margarita cannot win,
Not all the time, and time is his.

The children play games,
Singing happy songs and circling
In the "ring o' ring of roses"
Before all fall down.
In the car park, by the tram stop,
Gossips gather and raise their noses.
Stand around in semi-shocked poses.
Doors open, a boot lid closes,
The tram draws closer with barely a hiss,
As a mother and a father gently savour
                    A farewell kiss.

A forest walk down reality's path.

Walk through the pine forest
Where light dances with shade.
Twigs crack, birds fly, earth smells.
Needles grow until they fall.
Soft hands, stained hands, caress bark
In moments of joy, or displeasure,
In deep affection,
                            Or lifelong terror.
Through gaps between the trees,
The light and shade of love and hate
Plays soul-deep searching with the eyes.

There is no being alone in this wood.
They walk with you, silent, no footsteps fall.
You, with your emotional pricks, see them.
Some may go hand in hand,
Others turn their backs to avoid your eyes.
Some continue life, others fade or die,
But all stay defined
                            In the chambers of the mind,
Whose flood gates fail to hold back the tide
Of wet-on-wet paints that colour moods.

Colouring you, colouring the forest.

Enter a glade's scented amphitheatre,
Or face a frustrated turn into thorny barriers.
Inhale the combustible mix of
Air to breath and life's scratches,
That act upon your senses, triggering
The squib embedded in the stage
That turns costumes into
Dream-coats or straight-jackets.

Dance with Midsummer fairies around the ring
Or fly in the darkness with the deceitful Sluagh.
But, for better or worse, luring is a power
                                In life.

In the woods, where chimes hang from branches,
Moving with dings and chinks in the soft breeze,
Black bags swing in a distasteful dance,
As imagination seeks to fly free, unhindered,
The spirits prancing between the trees suddenly run.
The shadow-sound of footsteps crack twigs,
As the moaners and moral groaners of the modern world
Gather pace and volume, setting barbecues and picnics
                                Behind you.

What anger morphed into hate destroys

I have spoken to the rabbit in the moon.
She promises to keep you safe, sound
And whisper sweet dreams as you sleep.
When you wake, she will be unseen,
But there, high above, always watching.
Her watchful gaze will reflect love.
So simple, so easy, so free.
She will be bold in the full moon,
Maybe hidden in the crescent,
But there,
                  Always there
Surveying a world driven by transaction
And quid pro quo, She stands above you,
Expecting nothing, ignoring all rates of exchange.
The rabbit shines in what is freely given.
She takes the kernels of love
And grinds them into warm bread.
It is yours to taste.

But in that moment's blur
As you savour that sweet taste,
You gag on the sour.
You fail to sense the moment
Anger bites you.

Mix up in the weather

Grey skies and cold rain
Confuse St Valentine's Day.
Saint Swithin is just around the corner.
But sunshine and warmth
Has found a crack in the sky,
Opened by the flurry of wings
Of Aphrodite dressed in white.

The sky offers hope.
The wings can help flight.
And the clouds can part
To reveal the heart of the full moon
Where secrets lie
Conjured by the rabbit
Who never forgets you

Bad habit

Each time the joint burns out,
The glass goes down empty,
The kebab van pulls away
And the curry leftovers go cold,
Marks a milestone in 68 years
of bad habits.

The mystery of the unseen

You looked tired, I felt.
You said you were,
A hard day,
My arm found its way around your shoulder,
And, without a thought, I pulled you closer.

Together we stared at the sky
With sounds of joy and triumph
As another shooting star zips by.
A space rock, speeds overhead,
Narrowly caught in the corner of eyes.

Perhaps it was space hardware,
Placed their by science,
Or just the rip of energy
That explodes within the sky.

What am I missing? That tail of gas
On fire, the burning torment
That drives this simple sperm through darkness.
In search of an unreachable egg.

Untitled

White roses blooming in winter,
Defying the Devil's cold snap,
People squinting through telescopes,
Bought cheap for Christmas,
To follow wandering stars.

They cried for some new Messiah,
They implored new mothers
And checked family trees
For attached possibilities
Of righteous Hallelujah

They cried. They looked for a leader
By following the crowd.

There is the blue sky.
It sometimes turns black.
A finger points down.
Beyond its tip is the invisible,
Unforgivable,
Unreachable
Infinity.

Pick pocket playtime

All storytellers are thieves.
And, as thieves, they may lie.

Gossip stimulates,
And they may even speak truth,
But tell it backwards.

The masters and masturbators
Pick up their crowbars, and,
With jackboot determination,
Gruntingly lever stolen treasures
into play,
       Into words,
               Music,
                      Paint
And clay,
Setting shapes on sticks as silhouettes
For our eyes, ears, hands to engage with;
For our feet to tap to,
Our curiosities to sigh with.

Even small squares cuts from old party dresses
Pressed into a collage of secrets to tell a new story,

A story framed,
> To create a meaning.

A meaning may be meaningless to some,
But more for those who add their meanings too.

That is the art of something new.

Take the lies, imaginations, gossips and backward truths.

Take them all and add them to yours.
Through our merger of truths, lies and falsity,
Let us magnify beauty.

In the meantime,
Ignore this hand's secretive ten second search
Inside your pockets.

Sunglasses in the dark

Sleepless in a sweat stained night,
A time of anagrams and missing pieces,
Colliding circles twisting to spirals,
Like metal meeting metal on a motorway.

That crash hangs inside the head,
Behind the eyes in slow-mo re-enactment.
It was out of body, it was blank, it was hanging
Upside down, a reply lingering in mid-air.

A distorted look at mind-paintings,
Hanging out of square, they return stares
Of exhaustion. They too feel overlooked
By eyes hidden behind shades,
Some mirrored.
                Others polarised.
Many just a cheap protection
 That comes in *fancified* frames of flowers, hearts
And rhinestone to give children ten minutes
Of happy disguise, a memory before legs
Become twisted, lenses fall, left buried in sand.

The jewels of childhood left half-hidden,

In damp sand, trampled by bare feet,
Washed by a tide that comes and goes,
Goes and comes. Memories bound for losing.

Like the old funicular, up and down, balancing
One weight against the other. Riders sitting on
The long bench, always a dog at one end,
Tongue hanging out, shoulders moving, drooling.
Drooling for life, a simple bowl of water
Found in a complex world of questions.
I tried the Cairo solution for something to do.
Soak the bed sheet. Go under. Sleep, repeat.

But the sweat comes back with the twinge
Of a bite, mosquito buzzing in and out of range.
Stop burning the coffee powder, start drinking.
Add whiskey. Sleep has lost.

Reality is confused by repeated reality
That is the abstract nightmare, where
Scattered battlefields expose spongy innards
Soaked in blood.
Sagely, you nod your head.
Does that mean you understand nightmares.

A reference to Chapter 23 of Master and Margarita

Night shades drawn around the trees.
Bulging eyes pump and blink in the breeze.
Ropes hang loose, hang ready from branches,
Branches without leaves. Nobody leaves.
Nobody leaves a hanging without a little death,
And the coldness it brings, that chill that sings,
That haunts and sings some more until that second,
                              Something snaps

As we went down to the woods tonight
Inside the pathway of our dreams, it seems
To never end, that is how it seems, so that
Is how it is. Naked Margarita upon her broom,
Naked Natasha astride a pink pig. Bodies bristling
Within a cool night sky, Pan music and shooting stars.
And all want to kiss the right knee of Naked Margarita, as
Something snaps.

As ropes grow tight, upside down erect. As knots slide
Into that point of neck-snap, sacks of sin are being cut down,
Rotting in the forest mulch, seeping down through the crust
To top up wine barrels for the ball, the wine that turns to champagne,
Then brandy, then blood. Blood to bathe in, blood, blood, blood
To massage the body, the breasts of naked Margarita,

Blood to spurt like period fountains of example into Berlioz's head,
Something snaps.

Again, a snap, the same kind of snap of opening the lid
Of a head, a cup, a vessel to toast us all, a reminder of choice,
A false choice, an illusion, a trick of the Devil and God alike,
As out of the fireplace at midnight's snap, they walk,
Those victims of the woodlands, now walk into a timeless zone
That is not even theirs, just a space to fill as guests and that music,
That music so torturous, that torturous sound of sin and pain and
Something snaps

It snaps again, the cap of the vial half hidden in the bag of
Madam Tofana. She passes her bottle around with a smile.
Frieda walks, dropping her handkerchief again, and again,
Again it floats, carrying the waft of a salmon of second freshness.
With each ball that drags, each chain that clunks, you believe,
You believe you have a choice. You believe you have a choice.
Belief, choice. A false cross against the eternal laws
Something snaps.
It makes no difference, as, like a flash in the pan,
And after a ten second pause, a twig snaps,
elastic snaps, necks snap, snap, snap, fucking snap.
And evil begets evil.

That is the moment something has snapped.

Look closer

Look closely.
Stare and Stare harder.
Soon they will show themselves.
Those clever hearts,
Those foolish hearts.
There are plenty of hearts up there.
Some say they are covering the moon.
Others argue they are trying to reach it.
How enticing that half hidden moon is,
Using the magic of stage craft,

Some thought they had.
Now they are simply dropping away.
How enticing that half hidden moon is,
Using the magic of stage craft,
To pull rabbits out of a hat.
That false moon shines
A false light

Argue over significance and need, In this world we demand recognition
For the sins against us with our trespasses forgiven.
That simple recognition, the one tiny dot of the heart's demand.
This is not, as nothing is, about shining love and dark hate.
It never is. It is cannon fodder clouds taking metaphorical shapes
Reaching for a borrowed light that misleads all into unmapped infinity.

Eggshells

I tried not to break them,
Those eggshells that love laid before me.
But some days my feet refused to dance,
Or tip-toe along that stretching egg-shelled road.

My feet just could not compromise,
And stepping inside heavy boots
With thick, tyre tread soles, my legs
Would run, jelly-like weaving,
Without control.

Trampling fields of buttercups and daisies.
Using light and daffodil signposts, searching
For a new story to tell from some story chair
Made from paper mâché and headlines.

I was never driven by hate, love maybe.
But your eggs were blown,
Devoured of nature's promise of life.
And, in one snotty puff,
Normal was born.

The comfort of the curl

My eyes have felt yellowing bruises on your skin.

My heart has felt your joy of life within.

My brain.

My brain has turned numb with the contradiction.

Yet,

I dream.

And throw the torn-up papers storing written words to the wind

That carries the music that drains the pains and sifts the joys and

With a finger flick and push from a thumb, a click sets free

The numb.

Sing,

And as you sing

Play with your auburn curl,

Twirl it around you finger and let it spring back,

Into a curl.

Let your elfin Demelza drink ale and dance inside
                            Your hand-held-mirror,

Reflecting you barefoot atop the castle walls around

                      Your compassionate heart.
Go, skipping along the battlements, taunting
                      The temper of jealousies.
Set free the energy that curls in the pit of
                      Your gentle pouting stomach.
Take chancy leaps and stop split-second
                      Motionless in the air,

Gehüpft wie gesprungen,
Echappé,
Jeté,
Brisé,
Sissonne,

Defend with fierce strength, stand fast, stand firm
Against the doubters and non-believers,
Who do not see what they doubt or understand
What they do not believe.

You may feel pain.
Experience joy.
But never, I say never,
Let the numbness win.

"They understood only too well the liberation into savagery that the concealing paint brought."
– Lord of the Flies

She puts on her make up,
Then walks out the door.
Another wife gone.
Another girlfriend gone.
Another love lost.
I guess that's how it goes.
Love, comes,
And goes.
It leaves on the tips of toes,
Or riding on the sharp spike of high heels,
Or, with just a silent closing of a door.

It goes just the same,
Bitter or sweet.
Smart and neat,
Scruffy and ruffled.
Cool or angry.

We all have our different ways
To say goodbye.
And space in hearts have been warmed.

It does not have to go cold,
Like a morning after half-eaten fried egg breakfast.
I can love more than once.
And so can you.
Just say goodbye in this only passing of time.

A curl

Twisted fingers turning,
Hand combing through hair.
I really want to see you,
But don't know if I dare.
I really want to see you,
To sit in a chair,
And stare.
I want to watch you
Washing your hair.
Putting on make up
As you sit there,
On a piano stool,
As you wear
A loose towel dressing gown,
The type that slides off shoulders
To reveal your spine.
As you remove the towel turban
And shake-out your hair.
I want to breath to the rhythm
Of the stroking brush,
That pulls out damp knots,
The ones that tie me

To the vision.
All your concentration
On the mirror
That holds you inside.
Reflecting each facial pout
And lipstick kisses.
It's just a dream,
An image inside of me.
It's just my twisting fingers,
Hand combing your hair.

Through the wardrobe

Walking in wintry mist outside my door,
Through snowflakes, legs brushing
Tipping snow from
Weighed down, fragile branches.
This world some would say: This is Narnia.
This is magic. A window in a wardrobe.
A shut, frosted window,
but no exit out.

Just a panel that keeps the wardrobe together,
Added to keep a barrier between the realities
And the White Witch. To keep the pests,
Those mice, the cockroaches, barricaded out.
Only imagination can walk through it.
Only imagination can see
Snow on mythical horizons.

Gloves for hands that want to weave,
Stay on a shelf. The foreplay of necromancy
Is a woven spell with threads to spark into life.
Coats stay on hangers, leaving a figure naked,
Pressed against the seeping chill through compressed wood.
These hands, stiffened by frost's bite,

Want to touch.

They want to find a reality inside a dream.
Touch bare, warm shoulders of pale skin.
They want to come from behind and touch,
So a spine can be seen arcing from a finger's kiss,
So hair can freely brush a face
That relishes the scent inside softness.

A head bending back, balanced on a long throat
Where muscles stretch and swallow the moment.
Layered hair that turns into a gentle storm,
As the face turns its cheek to brush the free fronds.
A bare chest sighs to take
A balanced, feathered weight,

One of entanglement of a dream, of toes
That grip, knees that bend to the spermatic cord's shiver
Against the temptation of an apple-arse. An arse
That rises to meet each shudder that opens
The vas deferens door,
Each squeeze freeing the little animals.

They dance within the space of moisture,
Upon a stage in a palace of mystery.

A flooded palace where dams burst,
As each hand cups a breast, leaving fingerprints
To prove the reality
That sleeps naked in fantasy.

It is the fantasy whose calling card
Is marked with fragility, with a whisper,
Caught in the slight translucency of marble;
The living statue of visual depth, of skin
That has bonded, chipped
From a single block.

It is found in the wood layered with virgin snow,
Where footprints are pressed as tip-toe dents,
As if left by small birds that have flown
And flown away, singing whistles of relief.
A soul, a prince of faded ecstasy, presses his back
Against the back of a wardrobe. Scared. Too scared
To look out the window, to see if the statue of permanence
Still stands against the weather's wintry blast,
Or has run away with his shadow,
The only blanket he had ever owned,
That had kept him warm.

And so, finally

Fate, a neutral player,
Sits slightly squeezed in the middle.
Love is looking away,
Knowing the cause is lost.
Hate rubs hands with glee.

Fate is okay, it is what it is.
Love still cannot look.
Hate's hook starts to bite.

Through the portal sits the man.
A teddy bear, a shirt, a bra
Turning, twisted, stretched
Between his hands.
Held to his face
To catch the tears,
Muffle the groans,
Shuffle the fears of the fear.

His finger thick,
Stiff on industrial hands,
Knotted by a grip unready to let go,
Soft heart hardened as bitterness grows

And memories of love flow,
Draining the pipeline of history
Flickering like a film in his mind.

Those fingers, lined nails filled with grime,
Linger long on the unclipping of the bra,
The sensual exploration of flesh in hand,
The teddy bear won at the visiting fair ground;
The shirt? Where did that come from?

"Gotcha!" Hate was heard to cry.
Love turned away with a tearful eye.
Fate assigned the man below
To Hate, who assigned the man below
To Revenge, where hell fires glow,
To seek and kill the enemy,
To strangle with bare hands,
To kill, to kill the pain,
To kill and to kill again
On the front line of this battle
Between peace and war.
Hate, he refuses to catch the eye
Of downtrodden Regret
Who is standing by to move Revenge's pain

To a new level without gain,
To drugs, to drink, to internal despair,
Hate for them then hate yourself.
It is win win for Hate, his only care.

Love, looking into some broken mirror,
Knew there was no chance, but to follow
That same old pattern that hate inspires
In the world of rubble,
                              Of dust and phosphorus fires,
Of funeral fires that take empty coffins
Behind the curtain in the word of the world,
Where nothing is certain.
Nothing but the working man
With scuffed, calloused hands.

These are the hands that tied the knot
And hung the body outside the gates,
The ones that lead to hell or heaven.
But who will take his soul, this suicide?
Will it be Love?
Will it be Hate?
Can he survive the hanging knot's twist
The overdose or quick slash across each wrist.

His blackened face,
His dirty clothes,
A broken tooth,
A blackhead nose,
Who knows?

Love and Hate have called draw.
All is now in Fate's juggling hands,
It could go either way or so they say.
Despair will either let him go
Or keep him there.

                                       All is suffering for him.
Just a win or lose gamble for others.
This is the gamble for Love and Hate
As Fate plays his joker card,
Placing it before Despair
Who plays for false victory
With a bankrupt care.

A man, like other men,
Like women too,
Will go to war.
He will learn to fight,
He will learn with hate,
To kill from a distance,

To dance with death
In close quarters.

And if Fate's dice
Rolls and spins and turns up a seven,
He may survive.
Home he will go,
An empty space
And a head filled with memories
Only he knows.

But Love,
She may dance and spin
And pull out the Queen of Hearts,
That troubled card that loves to win.

As he walks down the High Street,
Looking for shiny shoe or two,
The old ones may walk him
Into something new.

Love may start a-new.
Hate, challenged, may well fall,
As he hears an optimist say:
"Love conquers all."

But there are tricks up every sleeve
In the space around the corner,
Where the tout plays with cups and balls.

And the pessimist says:
"Things cannot get any worse."
And the optimist replies:
"Oh yes they can."

There is no *and finally*.

E Major

Airlines and ticket sellers,
They would call me a frequent traveller,
One blown by different winds,
Steered by wheels and rudders,
Bored on those days of flat sails,
Damp, cold, and still.
Pumped by sun and moon,
Warm, romantic, blessed,
Time filled with rhythm.

I have crossed borders,
      I have crossed the Equator,
            I have crossed the centuries.
I can trade memories and adventures,
Like pirates on the South China Seas
Traded trinkets and slaves.
I have never ridden a magic carpet,
But I can imagine the sweep and swoop
Through ancient cities of Arabia
Where market-sellers bargain
And wink, and where the eyes of
Long-fingered pick pockets widen,

And, feeling the weight of a wallet,
Bare feet run, dodge, swerve and curve
Their way to some hidden stash.

I have never lived just one life,
But the life where I am at a given moment,
A given place, a tempting space,
Dependent on the company kept.
Who is there to meet, to see, to talk,
To swap experiences over coffee,
Over wine or beer, or arak.

Exchanges over the fine bone
Cups of saucer-balanced tea,
With polite fingers pointed.
Or, opportunities spotted over stolen cracked cups,
Eyes reading the leaves or the grinds. All found
In the spills and spoils of poverty and palaces
That sit at the junction of entitlement.

Inside my playful worlds
I escape the mundane I long for and deny,
In one breath, the parochial day of normal.
That longing to play Mumblety-peg chicken,
Suspended for a while, until the itches begin.

The husband, for example, wanting to use
His fingers at the dinner table.
The daily grind worker, moving motionless
Without protests, fearing the mortgage load,
With bills, dues and duties owed.
The birthday, family wedding, the car wash.
Of course, the children, playtime
And school time, games and exams,
The cut knees, broken arms. All,
At the very ordinary level of life,
I have found love.

    I found hate.

        I found my fragility.

Only to be saved by packed bags,
My tickets and entitlement to
The frequent traveller points system.

I have lived where it rains a lot.
A house with spare rooms,
A garage for two cars, and,
Around the dinner table conversed with guests,
With nods of approval towards a new Volvo,
A football score, and the secret gossip

On the garden step over a cigarette:
Who is sleeping with who, and
Who is getting divorced, and
Who is being promoted out of turn,
Or sacked. Everything comes in sacks.
They are in the sack together,
Presents come in sacks at Christmas,
Their home was ransacked by thieves,
The guns were not toys that pop,
The hunger was not just missing breakfast.

Sometimes the one world
With its own scale of love, hate
And sad fragilities damaged by borders crossed,
Cannot defend itself against
The multiple worlds where the scales of love, hate
And sad fragilities damaged by borders crossed,
Crumble into one another.
 And the one world gets sucked in.
And I get confused.
Which world am I in?
And there it comes,
The E-Major, deep, resonant,
Strikes the space, fills the space,

Grows in the space,
Fades in space to leave space.
More than one day makes a life,
And each day depends
On which world you stand in.

And, as you juggle the stirring movements
Of worlds, time, and physics, you forget
The importance of history and geography
That illustrate the stories of survival and change.
Underground tectonic plates creep, elbow and push,
Like a football crowd pushes against the barriers,
And your ribs ache, your breath tightens, as the dynamo
Cranks and turns and pushes energy through
The Planet's crust and the shaking starts.
Which world am I in? I have never stood in one world.
I have been standing too close to the edges, as
The Eurasian plate tussles with the Indian plate,
The Iberian Plate, north of the African plate,
Welds to the European plate, a bonding direction
That makes history and geography one.

As life stumbles around the subduction zones,
You reach the point of boiling.

In weariness, boredom, excitement, and drive,
In the face of poverty, in the face of riches,
In the face of your one world of comfort.
The zones you live in have their rules,
Their regulations, their corruptions
And their frustrations. In all worlds,
Love shares the food in the bowl, as
Hate steals the food from the bowl.
Fragility shakes the hand of wanting,
The fear of losing what you gained,
And then it rolls the dice that will
Shake the fate of all your winnings.

This dying fucking planet with sliding doors,
Trap doors, lava floors, shifting floors, shop floors,
football scores, Imaginary whores, garden stores,
All spinning around in a stillness taken for granted.
This surface world,
It cries with change, from rags to riches it never claims,
Sitting in space, turning on the looping sound of a single note.
Antalya, the perfect place for holiday,
Antalya, too hot, too hot, too hot to relax.
You love me, I love you, but my worlds are confused,
Confusing our world, confusing your world,

So you hate me, but I love you.
Am I expected to learn to hate you too?
At times I do,
In this place of unknown forgiveness.
No understanding. No recognition.
For those who plant their flag in a world,
The one and only one they claim as theirs,
Fragility scores the highest points.

Feet stand on a plot of needles and damage done.
Still, I love. So what? Who cares?
Love and hate are the studies of natural hazard risk,
The mathematics of togetherness, the science of falling apart.
But the arts and humanities, they belong at that point
Where edges crumble under pressure, and fragility's fountain
Spews forth its wavy line of purification and life.

Which world are you in today?
Is it the one where all is rules and condition?
Tradition? Your broad goals of ownership and pension set,
Your options of how to get there set.
Or,
Is your heart beating,
Your eyes shining,

As you start to shake.
As the ground shakes.
And you jump into a place where rules get broken.

Should you end in isolation,
Or boredom from too much,
Or should you step back,
Unable to leave one forever,
Join another and, or, juggle,
Be prepared to crumble.

I can be Mr Pleasant.
I can be Plastic Man.
I can walk down the high street
Of that space and smile.
Or complain.

I can be in plastic love
Or pleasant hate,
And in both I can be brittle,
Looking at how hot and cold
Change my state of being.

Sometimes that has been me.
But I prefer the joy of literature

Where mistakes make stories
And dreams, well,
>> They build
>> Glories.

E-major,
Synchronised and played on multiple pianos,
As the light plays towards the edge of darkness.
You, dear reader, have read this poem.
Maybe this whole book.
It is another day in the life.
Was it your life?
Or did you just watch?

There is strength in love and hate,
But once inside fragility, the choice is yours.
Emerge weak.
> Be reborn strong.
Suffer or learn, kiss or tell.

Someone much maligned and questioned for his talents,
Once wrote something along the lines of the world being a stage.
He also wrote:

The King's a beggar, now the play is done.

All is well ended if this suit be won,
That you express content, which we will pay,
With strift to please you, day exceeding day.
Ours be your patience, then, and yours our parts.
Your gentle hands lend us, and take our hearts.

The complexities of a life lived in motion,
Physically, emotionally,
In a world of infinite experiences and choice,
How do we define ourselves?
Not in choosing one world,
But learning to navigate the beautiful,
                              The painful friction
Where all collide.
There is no *and finally.*

www.ingramcontent.com/pod-product-compliance
Lightning Source LLC
Chambersburg PA
CBHW011127070526
44584CB00028B/3806